SKY-MAMMALS

Also by Blair Hamelink:

Ill Weathers & Other Fates (QuillKeepers Press, 2024)

SKY-MAMMALS

Blair Hamelink

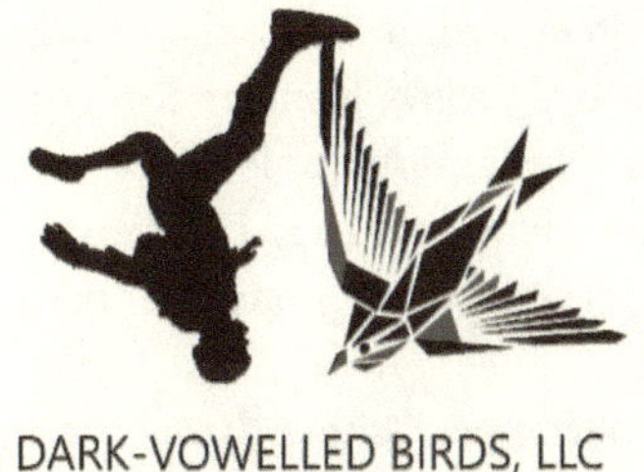

DARK-VOWELLED BIRDS, LLC

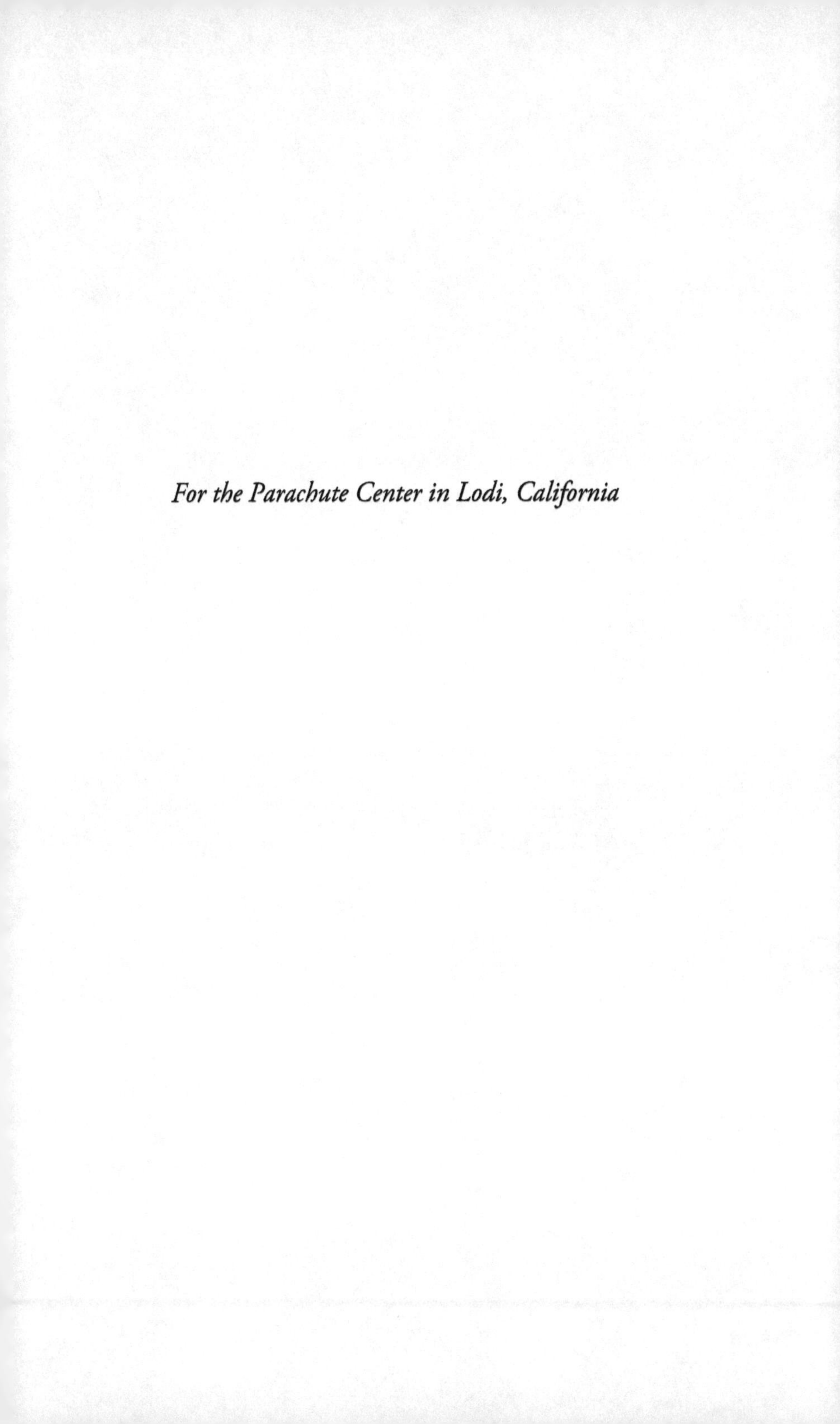

For the Parachute Center in Lodi, California

"When a man does not admit that he is an animal,
he is less than an animal"

-*Michael McClure*

Contents

Author's Preface

The poems in this book use skydivers as its muse. Skydivers are a group I have known well in the 17 years I have been active in the sport. They are perhaps a group best known for their revelings and self-proclamations of feralism and revolt. Of which, I, too, dabbled in, as I put that briefest flight on a pedestal. But, at some point, (I think, around jump number 15,000) as I started to gently decompose, I came to understand (or completely fabricated the idea) that the physical pain, and the fading zest I had been experiencing was conclusive of the triteness that is skydiving, that is simple, predictable, mechanics. Something that poetry is not. Jazz is not. And for some reason this realization warranted a certain poetry of velocity that corrupted my obsessions and this book.

Adrenaline first came to me in the form of *not-knowing*, as the unknown stimulus, potential of barely scraping by. A thrill similar to creation—where something comes out of nothing, but not quite. With the skydive there was never any "something coming out of nothing" it was merely a plaything of wind and dance, looming with mundane briefness; it was all repeat performances, improvising on the slightness of gravity. However, unlike jazz, each repeating performance was less and less convincing that flight is, in fact, a phenomena, and what a strange, privileged thought that is to have.

With poetry, during the process of a poem's creation, its trajectory is unknown—but with the skydive, it is a known science as imminent as throwing rocks. Therefore, in these poems, I decided to remove skydivers from the monotony of their actual, physical world—for its lack of magic—since the miracle of skydiving is in its sheer existence, in the knowing that it happens, and that the rules of nature continue to strive.

To write these poems I entered a mythopoesis where skydivers are more in touch with their animalism, detached from materiality, and acceptant of the mythic roots of the first freefalls—falls that were free of the whole hum-drum of perfect touchdowns and mathematical glide—that of Icarus and the Rebel Angels, where, the fall was a blank page, and where, a bardic romanticism glorified those paranormal endeavors.

In these poems, skydivers are an untamed species of mammal, living on the fringes of sky and ground; a species who have obtained a knowledge of the body, and a *gnosis* of the mysterious, beyond the physical. For these mammals-of-the-sky, the space they occupy is a turbulent blur; a dream-reality teasing perspectives that only Gods experienced. Their mission is to achieve transcendence within the hurl of terminal velocity—an absurd paradox: to reach heaven in the descent away from it.

Sky-Mammals are apprentices of Icarus, who evolved to embody the blue eyes of Napoleon, so, arrogance and delusion take root in their psyche. As creatures of habit and exemplars of Darwinism their survival is indebted to the courage of Icarus, the ingenuity of Daedalus, Isaac Newton's laws of motion, and Daniel Bernoulli's principle of lift; figures who helped shape Sky-Mammals into the creatures of the absurd which they are today.

Russian poet, Vladimir Mayakovsky, writes:

> it's not
>> with weapons
>>> the air is filled,
>> but with language. (trans. James Womack)

When Sky-Mammals reach terminal velocity they create a high-pitched cry due to the Doppler effect: $(f = (\frac{c \pm v_r}{c \pm v_s})f_0)$. A sound similar to the dropping of V-2 rockets in Thomas Pynchon's

Gravity's Rainbow: "A screaming comes across the sky. It has happened before, but there is nothing to compare it to now." But, to compare: the sound of Icarus falling, or of the Rebel Angels cast out of heaven. It is not weaponry in the air, it is the language of revolt. A revolt against the restrictions of nature. Michael McClure writes that, "the basis of all revolt is sexuality… the erotic impulse is to destroy walls." The walls are sound barriers. Poetry, as well as freefall, is a revolt, is sexuality, is a sonic bodily art that expresses emotions and desires, which, like words, "are physical parts of the body composed of infinitudes of tissues and nerves and actions of the body-physical." The skydiver's Doppler scream is a declaration of animalism and mortality. This absurdity, hysteria, madness, is a True animal process.

Mythologically, those first freefalls were failed flights caused by a flawed temperament that John Milton refers to as *disobedience*, or the fall of man. It was Milton's "Infernal Serpent and his host of Rebel Angels" who birthed disobedience in their eventual casting out of paradise. To be a mammal-of-the-sky is to be a vertebraic creature who has defiantly made home in the altitudinous spaces above; an archaic dream, and the ultimate disobedience. These poems infuse that archaic dream into the skydiver's contemporary world of ill-decision (a world that bears *so many* ills) to emphasize that, as Shakespeare writes, "conscience does make cowards of us all." That it was conscience and a willful rebellion that caused Icarus and the Rebel Angels to stumble upon the phenomena now known as freefall. A phenomena that has always lured the disobedient into a distinct fatalism that never seems real until it happens. Here, the surrealness of freefall comes to mean, *more real*—and the root of the words, *fate* and *fatal* are realized. Sky-Mammals live in the face of this; causing such temperaments to flare. My hope for these poems is to subtly reflect that socio-psychological aspect of the Sky-Mammal habitat, and like Milton, lean into the double meaning of the "Fall of Man."

I wrote these poems partly because I wanted to extend on Michael McClure's fascination with the mammalian desire, and partly as elegy for a paradise lost; a paradise that existed in California, and which was, an indestructible realm of light.

One comment I continually receive from first-time jumpers is that freefall feels *surreal,* as if it is like entering a new realm, and an abstraction from everyday science, where the expectation of an intense ground-rush doesn't come, and "afloat" seems our reality. Barbara Guest writes that she "grew up under the shadow of surrealism… where the arts evolved around one another" and where "poetry extended vertically, as well as horizontally." I rely on this sentiment in these poems, as my field of composition extends to the verticality of the skydiver's descent, where the abstraction of both freefall and poetry come together. Any first-time jumper will tell you that there is a moment during that first jump, where the mind is at odds, where one is in disagreement with everything they have been taught, where absolute truths are somewhat bent—and if, as René Magritte says, "the surreal is but reality that has not been disconnected from its mystery" then, Sky-Mammals are living the mystery, living in the illusion, where perhaps they are indeed, for the sake of this artifice and my own fabrications, some mammalian species of angel, or some other rebel, lost within the cause.

Rebel Habitude

Zephyrstorm & the Obsidian: a Landscape

elasticized beyond anvils is a sky,
is the soft colossus at bird-level,
& for a moment, the wandering
anonymity of us

laid open like a patient, the sun feeds us Hedonism—
beneath the sun, bathed in smaller fires
is the commonplace burn, is the bud's
abortive reap, abortive animalia

sprawled along this biology, the wind
follows the ringing from the jester's belled shoes
the wind: doom of trumpet-speak
is eerie upon ears, eyes, in hesitancy

in the tall grass: things found, the once vanished
pleasures; mobs of bone & lament

this mass
(once silent, under the cirrus invasion

under dark cocklofts, cycloptic plumes
in deep bosom'd mosaics)

is a collection of scars; healed, un-
healed, sprung from blue assemblies,

strung-out on kinesis & slope.

Pocket Aces

what rot taints this Newtonian Paradise…
what lies in its rancor, but remains of parade:
skydivers, jovially flung, dealt Pocket Aces
& an itch for that miniscule velocity on the cheek

the wind spoke with its devils,
we were free to dream of bare skies

that detritus heap grew & grew & grim-visaged-war
bunkered in the red flesh of my mouth

I choked on my words (so wrinkled, obsessive)
& mimicked the animal deity
                              in the guise of a Lion
adding desperadic vowels to the cacophony

beneath the faltering windsock, I sat beside my
mentor, he said: "big sky, little sky-mammals"

two feathers, in the blast of propellers,
pledge unwillingly to the doctrine of
the Now & the accident—(a wind-hive
ransacked of bulwark qualm)

the tetrahedron's poignant smile spun up my spine
where every single vertebrae became corroded
on its cord; the tetrahedron (the aviator's
indicator of fate) defaced me, unstoic in my center
as I went thru every longitude & latitude
of the bereaved words; words like,

rehabilitation (however orphic a plunder)
never was I sure of this Pride with its faint-like
consciousness & its gentle perplex

    (I tasted wild hormones at the diseased watering hole
                    I wanted to worship this world,
                        but I disdained the façade)

there were words, like the wind, like,
Aeolian muses—who were so luminous—to shuffle
bone & discipline with Aces & Kings

the timing always had me somewhat nonplussed
with its blasé immediacy

moments of folly in the fall were measured justly
there were no clocks of knavery, only
finality of landscape—

it was either Earth, or the cocksman of Zephyr, who
informed me thus: *I am in love with Eternity's*
terminal transition—
but Earth, you're so full of ghost-steps
& all I have is my majestic pirouette
but just as you instructed, I dismissed
yesterday's casualty
(the blitzkrieg debris clotted in muscular airs)

I said, "Earth, you've been pretty good to us so far
watching our evangelical strut, our sonic-flair,
its streetability—& our sinister desire
to leave you   with stockpiles of
pinpricks in the aftermath…"

& she replied, "Know that angels will sing you to rest
whether you fly with grandeur, or *de rigueur*—"

those words came closer, came quiet
I believed in the music of those words,
allied with a barren nature & sober
I believed in the silence & its undoing
I believed in the gaps
where I was dealt the loot

    (now, o' glorious summer,
    now you show me
    the healer, the pollinator
    ceaseless in the soil, sleeping
    (an epiphany like the empyrean beware
    & a seasonal salute to this glittery pot))

    now, I sit & observe
    stolen moments, amid
    dreadful dimensions

& for now, my pockets weigh me down
with tiny bottles of gin & stacks of aces—

those aces love to intrude my body, as the dirt
assumes a devil—my fate
gone across that rigid horizon
blows with authority,
with a ripe, knowing
certainty,
kept to itself.

Sapphire-Throated Rhapsody

at the dawn of our technological advances
 a mistake was heard in the turbine *grahhrrrrr*

the primatial animus with the bourgeoisie shoes
 celebrates the I of urge; [the prettiest birds:

yellow warbler
scarlet finch
sapphire-throated hummingbird,

entertain our days, harmonizing
the melodies of "Revolution" & "I Saw the Light"]

Aerialists, cobalt-pearled in the blast of engines,
 fly with precision & fluency,
 bound to the tedium of glide-ratios—
Dear Kingdom, can you hear the violinists squeal?
—sounds like,
 (a gravitational insistence)
 can you hear the audience
say: this show is puffed-up
 on primary color

this has now evolved into a business
of hoisted smiles
painted clownish,
 betrayed by spinal disease,
 age & gadgets
& reaching for a soul in the mirror

our affections
        were routine
        & our goodwill was so cheap
     but I have to say, I adored myself, I adored my
   contribution to the "V" flock—how we moved so
      matter-of-factly, like clockwork
& felt at home in the scream of the quack-tide—

but in the sapphire-fog… we became estranged
under the bell's
        incessant toll

            for us mammals-of-the-sky,
     opportunity roared
            in the turbine *grahhrrrr*
              & we refused the possibility for art,
          sang the same ol' love song
     the same rhapsody:

              blue this, blue that,
              sky, love, freedom…
                blue this, blue that

            —at the apocalypse,
                  the self in the mirror:

        long hair

                  blowing

     in the wind.

Blue-Eyed Napoleons

so, with irises implored
we've gone astray
            with bird-like-machinery
        gone astray
                into some marveled delirium

        as the airplane engine's
                belligerent grunt
    coerced self-deceit
    the body & the mind
                    was lured
into a world of militant freedom

            the exhausted gasoline…
            poisons the flown
            —it is a nectar so goddamn sweet

            & so sweet are these dreams:
    winged of white lightning
winged of circumstance
        & pomp—

            un-winged upon a
            righteous thwart

            (when they crash
    you can feel it burn
            you can feel it sting
    at the hub of the wing)

                    those blue eyes claim greenness
               in a "propeller   hypocrisy"
                    devoted to Earth,
               laughing at the base of the pyre
     where fossilized embers
                         drift   (monuments,
                                   out of reach)

          that airplane, that All-Day-Bird,
        drops bodies   (stubbornly,   chestly,
     malleable)   the lust that started at the
     mouth
     has spread over limbs

& sometimes, the (perhaps) bodily need un-
fulfilled, falls short

     figurations: figurined
               fallen for the Napoleon clause—
          merciless flight
eager & cursed
               in jolts of crazed emphatic yearn
          loyal to the abruptness
                    of the sudden-esque;
     the flight,
flawed by the cockily
          thrown

(& I know, in quarters of
weather—of a certain
brutish absolve—how un-
welcoming an angel,
or, jukethrob-like push—)

the landscape, it stretches
    from our feet
  with such a trite
        greeny
        giddyap & cog

        (& I know the dirt
        & the wind that it spake with
        & I know those corners
        of silence // hazard cones
        how they are aligned
        how they were manufactured
        under grim-eyes—by makers of
        a hefty warn)

& at the top of our summer,
    a (bereft) dialogue
  filled with
        distant insanity,
                    that is,
            Earthly refusal,
        a communique of specific form:

        pow
            & shun—
  roam & neglect—

            ((a detective asks questions
            among this sleep,
                this stumbling—))

                the orphaned are always
                   so provoked by dust,
             by da Vinci's bootlegged blueprint,
       remnants of the Demon's Rum on his breath
                      the Demon's Rum (liquid
              antagonism) disguises itself
                        camouflages itself
                    tastes angelic on the tongue
                angelic down the throat
                stirring cause & effect
                with promises of a
            pure,
                   heroic girth—

          that mysterioso,
                   that enigmatic whisperer,
             appears on the protagonists shoulder
        & points to the crater, where
                     the dust-ring halo
             still hovers
          above the loitering ghost…

             ["thou comst in such a
             questionable shape!"]

       —elegiac notes
                  tremble on the tongue

               & the bright pigment
                       in those eyes
          hold in the burden
                     of a smug volition
                  // a smug reality

(creatures of idiom
        in the sky
            in fleets of slow glory
            punctuated by
            an exclamation (!)

    (impugn equations
        of force—)

    they are, immersed in euphoric expressions
                of their entire beings—

                    figurations:
                            immaculately keen
                                    & shy

            are, so intimately visible.)

Lioness

a toothy creature,
mischievous
        eaten away on the inside—
            clutching to the fatty part
            of chaos; those eyes,
        inhabited by
            condemned-ghosts,
            smiling
                at the earthbound &
        hanging onto her little secret:
                    that she can already
                        fly—

            a-gape
            at the megalopolis
        of the angel-factory
I witnessed her
        convulsive shift
    from nowhere
            to the churn of skies,
    until, a gale force blew hard
        & her paws grew empty;
        that labyrinth, now
                tumbleweed—that paw print,
            (a *memento mori)* for this
    cumbersome memory:

            at Big Sur,
        nature begged us to be free
    & we pretended to drown,

we floated face-down
on the rippling surface
                    (in preparation)

wild horses circled her
    charismatic shrug
as she became the storm
    & I stumbled in those new shoes
Mama gave me
    guided by that
            languid snarl,
that languid snarl
    led circuses
        down HWY 1,
    following the oceanic hum—
        the purr of her
                habitation;
            searching for
                that faded print
        in the sand.

A Win(d)some Dedication

for the one with quiet eyes,
half-fledged & adrift
you, who made a stealthy glide
toward somewhere
inside yourself

in your raw youth,
you made wings
out of what you had been given:
Meat & Consciousness—

& hand-in-hand at the altar of wind
you whispered: *I do*, & were confined
to the blue background

there is a mysterious power
that sits within
& directs your nimble flock
toward vigilance

(born naked, out of fetal-
contemplation of ghost-
songs within dream-
visitations by the pink-
skinned bird, perched on some *laissez-
faire* branch
of the morality tree

     where snake eyes hiss
     at your strife

        at your face
        dealt with a consequence)

you recite sophic tales of intoxication
to an alternate ego
named, "the insidious wind"

(& you say that your meditations
                        are tranquil—)

& coming upon the miracle
        you hold your breath
        as you hear the sound
coming from
the opera singer's
        pursed lips

& you are

                oppressed by curiosity.

Lumbar Multifidus

this gathering of lumbar; a rubbish
of pardoned spinal cramps & body-whispers
sunk in hours of another tethered petering,
flicking through the A-Z of anatomy

this is a carousel
a jester-crowd foisted by the sun-of-what
with distaste & a hinge or a croak
bled & salvaged for the nexus-lash

a soul with a prey in its mouth, youngness
in its teeth & aches in its tracks (known for its
spiraling, shouldering,
wormish sway) laddering into skies

it's the damnedest thing—
how skies squeezed out selves ripped from such
brokenness—selves, starved
by the pipe-dream

& with particular curriculum: a sharp black
twinge & sleep—what or who laid down
this law; this parallelism, this courage of
arms & legs, eyes & smiles, muscle & bone,
so irked.

Flight, in Memoriam

so shone the orbic light—
we were indebted to the expanse of it
to the harp's melancholic etude
to its perfect measure

with eyes turned skyward
the dream, highly problematic

a noise from above
opened wings
into a mammal abode
of blossomed spines

the intrusion, soon to perish
in the slippery grace of blueness

perusing the liability waiver
(& the cunning of its savior-stanzas)
we signed a treaty with velocity
in the whirrs of turbulence

there were things we craved for
too far of reach & wicked—

knowing what we now know
of ruin & causation
the disjunctive syllogism:
if (a) (to be flung is to be famished) is true, then
(b) (to be flung & satisfied) cannot be true

—do you remember Tom Petty's
Damn the Torpedoes,
where it was suggested that even peasants
could walk with kings?

our escape loomed,
as if, a stellar-seethe
its final curveship
settled into a skyish surge
(where lay, this catalog of
archetypes: the same,
not miraculous, creatures)

the image in its stillness is more appealing
than the actual movement
this apparatus is sometimes antonymic
of the word, *Bliss*—
but at other times: I see Saint Mark's ferocity,
felicity, & the evangels risen (they look so familiar)

& as we say goodbye, as we,
the manipulators of wind,
say goodbye—
the black sky sits in its attic
with its odor of plaque-abyss,
tonguing the brim
of the dreamer's dream

& we hid, we wrote of a pure paradise: a place
uninterrupted by the foulness of weathers

we do not want our famine
to be the ought of confusion

we do not want our flingings
to be neo-religion
we want generations to sketch
the unhurried Revolution
scrounging around for the
most Holy torque, or the sabbath-sleep

adieu, adieu, to the pernicious hours
this obsession with being rescued
surely has passed
& I know there is
                    singularity
because I saw the poet
labor in her diphthongs
calling for a time-out

calling, or dangling
from the exactness
of the memorious sky
with its clouded posture

abdominously
loved in vain

these eyes, turn
skyward—

in our mortal coil
a bitter taste of adrenaline
that hint of dopamine
lives in our mouths

the taste of flight.

Aeolian Woe

Nose-Dives

of our mammalian desire,
which lives in the famed lurch,
guilty of tumult—I sing
(…so we enjoy our humanity—) however tedious,
while the Buddha (a cumulonimbus)
hangs like a bardic aside
mouthing the concepts of *upādāna, taṇhā*

I'll sing for us in our memory of paradise
where we were mere practitioners
& filled up on the cause by the gallon
& made the most of our fuel while it was cheap

they say that, skydivers (young Hamlets
in the Anthropocene) never say goodbye,
only see you later—puffed up on diatribe
& sloth, we romanticize the waiting
with an idleness among these
conditional symptoms:
rotation-sensitivity, momentus-troth,
axis-amalgamation—as addicts
of the unblest allure

& I thought that, if only our
range of vertebrates
might curl up to the animal sleep
& shuffle off the dream,
then we might dispose of our giant
windmill fantasies—

(in that sub-terminal haven, we found ourselves,
we fermented egoic seeds with eyes possessed by the
flowering melanin of swagger)

engines took us higher
parachutes left us alone
in the apex of solipsism

we understood what our compliance meant
yet, searched for some kind of rationale
in that fabled swoop
fear only appeared in urgency
under the thumb of a tendency
to want
(to participate in tragic passions
& risk becoming the corpse of desire)—

trickery was her most extraordinary quality
especially for those of us
dependent on her movements,
dependent on revels, gone amok

when our crusade was at its most narcissistic,
I stepped aside, I said:

> *I am not wind, but*
> *passenger; contender of*
> *delusion & death*

they call us drunkards of swine & heart
baffled at the height of our *I know, but* statements...

our attribute, not exactly loyal to the cause

our merrymakings, fraudulent
& Hamlet, as the opposite of say, Homer
had in him something dormant—
like how we burden the continuation
expectant of the wind to pick us up
& carry us

& the truth being:
given the perfect opportunity to slay
first we must make sure that the camera is recording
so that there is some evidence of our heroism

moles are a difficult protuberance to be rid of
(sometimes beauteous,
sometimes cancerous,
sometimes we scratch at them,
slice upon them with our knives
& place the removed piece of ourselves
in the center of our palms
& we're always drawn to the familiarity,
the feeling of looking at ourselves, admirably)

we are guilty to go from the pleasured dirt
to the shrewd bitten air,
calculating jumps like dollars
never starved of abundance;
nothing on the conscience,
not even carburetor exhaust

the challenge for our anthropology
is to tone down the masquerade
& let it fade, into a quietus brood

when I was a boy & I was stoned
I sat upside-down on the furniture
& imagined what it would be like
to fall like those Rebel Angels—
but when I awoke, arrows curved
toward me, breaching my
well-developed poise

& so I found myself suspended by fabric & string,
angled earthward, raising the leading edge,
exercising a trust in the mind,
making the flightline absolute—
(the arc to grant Salvation)

I pondered that curven reign of systems,
of ascension,
domination,
frequencies, oscillations—
Daniel Bernoulli's principle of lift, which sez:
the air that curves around points A & B
(dichotomies of resistance & phenomena)
are only attempts at the pivotal epoch

how is it that the arcs perpetual leveling
was opposed by bloody deeds?
the hazarded seizure of our world,
mad at the recurrence of energy
& pressure—
how did we contrive of such slants?
were we all incapable to say no
to the influence of whim?

I cannot speak of solution…

I can only theorize,
I can only speculate,
as in a painting on the
temptation of St. Anthony…

poor temptation,
you spent so long coiled in craters
you spent so long in the bottle,
imitating the immortal
counting all the things before you
while the whole world was still,
& you decrypted its flats

[I question the self-slaughter of parachutists,
where a three-pronged approach takes place:

1—the vision: reflections of the self
on the surface of water, grazing the silverscape
to ride it 'till flags & applaud

2—the decision: calculations amidst the
thermal turbulence that quivers;
knowing the thousand smiling faces, knowing
the way they peel open & slam shut

3—the execution: to follow thru with parachute as
weapon, heroic & stately, completing the gesture—
(…& then we pretend to be surprised
by the glossary of fallen names
spilling out of our brains, eruptive like petals)

& they ask, "does the Earth go to I, or I to the
Earth?"]

at the precipice, is a world, irreproachable
where giggling arms & legs & the elephantine skip
move as one
the pinnacles (smiles I defied)
play again: the wimpish descent
the descent, the descent, purgatoried
by condition
& the fandango
(fascinated only by
reflection & conquer)

—but the reality lingers…
that distant surface,

so prominent,
so irresistible.

Naked & Fallen

Naked, the descent of figures are
              sung in science
                 marks on the blackboard:
           the proverbial arch
         the source of song: Beelzebub's secret chord
               the rhythm: medium cataclysm.
Who, but the naked,
                 with their nasal weep
              expelled for angelic gumption,
         hesitant of that biblical slip, of Newton's
law, that signature of
              chance-murder-prophecy. Half-born-
         Boddhisatvas of hypoxic pitch, drifting
               thru the gates of an E(x)ternal
Paradise
           perchance to dream
         & in the dream
what terror—unfashionable heap of injury
         piled beside horizons,
           full-flown,
         amorous
              & Hamlet-hearted in hangar-alleys
           betwixt the alarum of Milton's lost key—
                 exiled from Paradise for talking
privately of
   boredom, the Grand Inquisition,
              Kane & Abel,
                 brethren of the corkscrewed wing.
         Who, but the treacherous
                    terminators of havens

falling into the abyss
                of a sexless
                              vortex, glorious
                      in its whirled arrival.
       Who, but those altitudinous animals
              orbiting within pleasures of the
         body-impetus
    in a domineering windscape,
    a snake-like sin, tax
                      'd by skies
              —infantilized arrows do-si-do-ing
the margins—mewling at the
         galore of space-time
            in a confetti storm of feather
                   apprehending body & wind
                   & the open mouth
                      on the shores of Hell
            disappearing thru a mass of dust,
                              thru the gust
       of some magma-front.
Who, but the rebellious, stripped of all mobility,
            something like dread in a wintery sky
                      clung to the backboned wing,
         un-
            sprung—
                      angel-headed-heathens in
                              depths of Eternity,
    finally fallen, stripped of sentiment,
                   stripped of reason,
                              of surface
    at the skeletal edge,
            holding embers of a life,
                              jestful & achy.

Moloch's Fingers

it seems, the battered arch
has indeed succumbed
to the capital scheme; all those aerialists
sucking up to the trend, to consume
momentum & cloth
Moloch's bloody fingers
under the sewing needle
pricked, made captive to the dream
where it's the all or nothing of the bright kingdom—
the filmic rise, the ooze-bait of pasts,
wronged us
in the instant replay—
in a fogged aperture, impatient
& Oliver-eyed, sinking out of the rapture
in elegant threads: navy, charcoal, turquoise & lime
Moloch's vertical roar
ridiculed our skyishness
while the Olympus-prodigal-son
hid in flamboyant Colosseums,
hemming his shadow,
stitching together ambition & fantasy
unaware that the real merchandise is time,
(semi-quavers, slipping thru the
hourglass, hellbent
on the epistemic clustering)
—time, like another
sort of thrust, like the perfect
million particles,
queued-up, anticipating
materials of combat & fray.

Sortie D'urgence

There is no noise like the slamming of a gate
& its proceeding silence. It took an engine, it took
ghostly correspondences & oil & an in-
comprehensible dynamo, to burst the scene
all those phony laughings, dwindling
all those elite *yeehaws* in our mid-air
imprisonment. Locked inside an array
of happy thunder; gravitation's dashly
persuasion, all fraternal & pith.
Our own private California with
dystopian insides & gorgeous plague.

Of course, we tried to challenge prosperity
& the dictatrix behind the convex lens.

Our paradise,
walled by politics, by physics
(we came into the world as creatures of
amphetamine & sacrificial attempt,
eyeing the goose
that laid the golden egg
& the mirage of the neon exit sign).

Never did I need to invent an escape,
it was always right there:
the sunset—
all we had to do
was glide.

"Why escape paradise?" They asked as we
caressed our spines, laying down the
felled who destroyed us
in the newspapers.
They spoke of impurity & doom
with a *what-for* gulp,
& I spoke of resurrection
with illimitation & imagination.
"That's not what dying does," they said.

I saw Saint Maurice of the bare-knuckled-academy
curse into the sky
all rebellion & air—"is there any
hope for us?" I asked.
& the exit was clogged with an abundance of tragedy
& the exit was all hither-tither
& the exit was a meaty mouth
full of broken teeth. Neither here,
nor there.

It was said by the bonfire,
that a merry glissando will be heard
as one glides away from this lifestyle of
toil & suave,
adrenaline & repent,
with nothing to show for it but
the thousands of ticket stubs
& stomachs swollen blue.
Now the itch has come back as a growth
& it's dour at the edge
of this turbined scheme,
as I try to look away from our famine.

I threw that dog-eared manifesto
into the moshpit
& saw the vast eternity
choke
& the exit was all
enterprise & glyph
& I ran around
with havens in my mind
as the responder of myth
with dreams of dreams
of the exit.

Now there isn't any penetration to fathom
only slipshod & qualm.
With shrouds of mercy
& jars of snakeoil
I set out against the door
against the rhombus memorial
all white-flagged with sordidness.

I failed to reacquaint myself
with the mural of our masters.
My chaos sold down the line
where my propulsion & strife
are chemicals
evaporating in a lucid sky.

& should our paradise
reoccur
somewhere else
with the cry of the morning cock
I'll still be imagining
that hunk of butter on a sill.

Rites of the Flung

under the miasma: vertigo's
descanted fling—

& shooed out from those
coughing machineries
devoted to the celestial chug
& astral feign; there, insofar, in the
beginning eons of a second wind
I was…

I became a pilot of the flung,
caught in a portion of peril

our blue occasion: bankrupted
by that odd scrimmage
& sometimes-swivel—

yes, I laid plots, I foretold sky-
dwelled riddles
            to the tenderwinged

            destined to obey
            the puff of Spring
            (a fricative music,
            ad-libbed meteorology)

            I saw the best wings
                    of my generation
            discarded in dustpans

forced into the hollowing
institutions,
rudely stamped

those ecclesiastic wings
slipped away

—left grooves in our
tired,   beaten   landscape

I stood with a shovel resting on my shoulder
     shirtless, wading thru
          swamp & yellow grasses

               inept & drunk on spite
I stood with a shovel
resting on my shoulder
feeling the pulse of common folly

so came a ringing of bells
& there stood:
               my tenderwinged students
               looking up   facing their ally

(who knew what the starvation proved?
—compelled by the structure
of romance, of an age-old contradiction:

     the indecent
               weathering,
     the weathered
                    perfection,

the perfect rise,
the perfect fall

               —a cuckolded phantasma)

I stood with a shovel resting on my shoulder
    (& gave up on my litany)

 & my tenderwinged students…
they spoke of

          the gallant aerial odyssey

with a bullish poise.

Dark-Vowelled Birds

there's a screaming in the sky—
inside a glass prism: a rainbow

tidal waves of dust dance above a myriad
of earthly dents—chaos & order echo the

cloistered flight; in a world of mostly in-
nocuous rhythms, there are those, intolerable

with daggers as smiles, mammals graze a sky,
self-emphatic, galvanic, facing scorpions—

some birds monitor this tender-loined-world
with eyes of the mournfullest hue,

with lumps in the thorax & broken teeth
spat onto the dirt—those birds call out

(such a mundane equation):
force equals mass times acceleration.

Wild Iris

above the center of the world, the airplane
engine stings your floral ecology

you, who have witnessed the span of mammal ir-
realities: the thousand breaching orcas

that once lived in my forehead & hissed from theirs;
Elizabeth Taylor's violet iris sprouted-eyes

radiating at 24 frames per second; Van Gogh
at the Saint Paul asylum painting from memory

your selfsame beautiful, jaded buds;
all our failed modernisms

evaporating into a fine residue,
our genus into the gloomy haze of ex-

tinction, our desolation riding along
the fossil-fuel of a mechanical wind.

Avowed

bewitched, bewildered,
I am, by her
the seductress of the leisured fall
her reddened aura
barbed in vacancy
she boldly snaps the bow,
bestowing the trivial wink

together we slept in a Buick '66 Skylark
among echoes of slurred somniloquy,
strung-out as Shostakovich's
"Jazz Suite No. 1,"
softly played

I was staring at my hands,
watching those
      white spots
      on my hands,
grow into fungi

riding those highways
we were inside the music
disguised as centerlines
& the endowed whoosh

when I heard the clarinet crescendo,
I was reminded of the Latin,

    fatalis & *fatum*

our occupation,
ignored
our therapy, cut off
as the pariah
paraded her barbarity

biting my lip on the edge
of a moribund wind,
she told me that
the song is not a song
but a movement of
torque & command

Amor Fati, she said,
stepping into the insidiousness

Amor Fati lit up on every
neon bar sign in sight

obligated to that bent verticality,
a dwindling inertia—

the homebound dove escaped us
(I think she loves to humor us)

in the disgraced silence
of the final movement,
I regarded her again;
her synonyms:

     valorous,
     stout,
     magnanimous—

she neglected to teach me about
the lovelessness of dirt
& how to deal

(just handed me a forty
with a courteous nod)

we raised the stakes,
raised the pot
to the price of exile,
rolled the die onto the dashboard
& went back in

(the descending arcs of our deeds
engraved on our retinas)

soon to be totaled
on the shoulder of Interstate-5,
near HWY 12,
we were at our
wits end,
where even shadows hid
in the 2/4 bounce of balladry
& spurned the time when we were
bridled & assured

no matter where we went,
we lived beneath those arcs
no matter how I tried to escape,
I felt her breath,
a constant liaison
in my ear

as she squeezed my hand
under the calamity
of a thousand auric moods,
& we stood alone

        avowed
to that

abandoned,
voodoo highway.

Beast of a Feather

i.m. Michael Suter (1977-2010)

Gargoyle Wings

slap it on me, bro, you'd say—
sword-voiced in the ink parlor
the Ace of Spades bleeding-edged
in a type-faced wreckage of flesh
for you to front & to freight

but your back was bare
pale white, but muscular
to hold up your head
& all those teeth

the space on your back
reserved for gargoyle wings
that space on your back,
stayed bare

but no one can say that
you didn't have wings
(wisdom-wings
in the flight of your voice)

as I walk this Earth
you soar above my shoulder
(my own Virgil
with the gargoyle grin)

the cry   of your swoop

                so distinct.

The Rest of You

& so, walking the deadest of streets,
as the sad-eyed vagabond of Dunedin
box of beer slung over my shoulder
—*DoubleBrown*, NZ's finest
walking the exact path as the
recurring spider in my dreams

& you, tattooed beast Jesus sky-punk,
dabbled in your flight
you on the west coast,
me on the east,
separated by that winding alpine road
(remember I traveled that road
under the lore of *Aotearoa*
(the heed of *Ranginui*,
      our Sky Father)

& I heard the birds, warning me,
but I chose not to listen

those Dark-Vowelled Birds,
warning again & again,
of the sea, of the sky,
of the ground; the cold hard ground
where you left us
& where the icy wind still blows…

I watched those birds
from my greyhound window
they followed me, as they always have

"

I shook your hand at the bus stop
you were like
a wise old prophet
                fringed with the white light of gnosis
yet, you called me guru—& I called you beast
& the beer on my breath laughed in your face)

•   •   •

September 04, 2010: Fox Glacier, New Zealand
propeller winding up to its capacity,
jet fuel in your nostrils
tail number: foxtrot uniform 24

what taste of flight
what last *little* taste of flight
looking skyward,
        looking skyward,
                & looking earthward

& looking
        & looking
                & looking

at that
hole in the ground — a hole
                in me

a hole   in New Zealand
        a hole
                        & in that hole:
                                an airplane—
        & those screams,
                        gone into a diminished silence

& there I am

                        I am the worm.

I am the worm… you disturbed my bed
I am the worm crawling the cold hard ground
I am the worm that escaped the bird's beak
only to be greeted by tail number 24
                        in flames

unscathed, I found myself lying next to a bone of yours
—your only remains
seeking comfort in the proximity
of your marrow

            once we made shapes in the sky
            our final shape in pieces in the dirt

            (& the sea, the sea,
            the sea still shakes
            moving sounds along the coast,
            spreading your final grunt)

I lost your Oakleys in the L.A. surf
in the Gulf of Thailand we left our old selves
to stumble out of that opium den
with angelic frolic & tincture

& you, pastor of the wetlands,
Fox Glacier's hero idol saint
with the sea singing your sermon
in a crashing cymbal splash

the birds are crying…
                    looking for you
—the rest of you

but now, my haka is deprived of your thunder

> *HE AHA TE MATE*
> *TE ORA*
> *TE ORA*
> *TE MANA TAPU*
> *KI TE RERE*
> *KI TE TIHI O TE WHENUA*
> *AROHA O TE ORA PAI*
> *TE ORANGA PAI*

& the sea, brings us back
& the sea, brings us back
to that same drop of water

the drop of water
that drowned those flames
on September 04

the water we sailed; the water that
belittles our pratfall & flop

& the water that gives life
& you are the ice melt that drips
                    off of Fox Glacier
& you move down the Fox River,
    down the Cook River
    & into the Tasman sea

                & I step my feet
                into those cold waters.

Cemetery Birds

burgundy coffin with the gold mesh
& portrait of you sitting perfectly still

inside: fragments of you
jigsaw bones & your damp shoes

whatever pieces of you those worms couldn't stomach

(how you escaped the blue background,
we still don't know…)

   & I am walking. I am walking thru the streets of
           Taranaki where you were born
        walking past the concrete gargoyle,
curled on the steps of the library where you once read

walking past the fellas in a classic pub brawl,
in honor of you

     & the birds at the cemetery gates
          in biblical quietude
        in lonely confusion
           perched in unease

  I'd like to think that
  in time—

        they'll fly.

Transcendental Velocity

An Open Letter to Icarus

Dear Icarus,

I have dust on my wings. I can't stop thinking about
my dream & the sting I felt in my shoulders
throughout my naked descent.

I wonder if you could smell burning hair as I have.

But much has changed since your father's day
our wings don't grow like feathers
they grow like vertebrae
       & then they ache.

Our materials developed
you should see what we have invented in your name!

Really, it was the mathematicians who saved us
& it will be our psychosis that kills us.

We hear the banter of airborne phantoms & think of
your fall. It must've been so loveless. So disturbing to
watch your technologies disappear. I feel that. In my
propeller hypocrisy I feel that.

I know there was thrill in your final roar. I dreamt it
& I felt something like bliss on top of the world,
while reality was a distant curve of soil & I was numb.

I couldn't feel the wax melting into my skin
because there was no wax.

Just an old-fashioned loathe,
an old-fashioned quest for more time, more
dissolve in the puddle of Spring

        at the brim of that tingle & sweat,
that shadow & fade

& you came to me with a handful of drenched wind
& a heartfelt nod.

You told me that some things are only disguised as
pleasures.

You told me that some things are very convincing.

That sometimes we feel that we have nothing left to
lose.

But, of course, we have everything left to lose…

& when everything is lost, somehow, there'll still be
more to lose.

I think about what it must be like to be face-to-face
with a consequence as you were. Almost like when the
phoenix's attorney is in negotiations with that skull in
his palm, reciting soliloquys in solidarity, watching
the briefly resurrected phoenix disappear in the sky.

(If I was spared, why?—oh, how I saw it coming…
the universe saving me—those bejeweled hands
cupping the small of my back—how I saw the arcs
move with occultic scream)

Icarus, I still don't know if I was saved, or if it's all in
my head…

You taught me how to accept the law (that Truth is a
vector equation & a formula to riddle the
imagination) & that going beyond limitation &
temptation was part of your foresight. But now, they
are piling rubber wheels onto the pyre & singing love
songs & I don't know what to do…

Now, they've built this machine; they've thrown
money at our love. It's true, I am in touch with my
mammalness. I've admitted mistakes. There was a
time when I couldn't dance. That frustration
reminded me of you. It reminded me that in this
dream, I have no control, as you well know.

But after all this time living in these pastures of wind,
I find myself being spiritually drawn to the dirt. I
hold it in my hands & it blows into my face. It is
speaking to me, but I don't know what it is trying to
say.

I thought I had an enlightened intuition—
(but sometimes my intuition was wrong,
as I found myself fighting with consciousness)

In those moments of Now, you cannot fight it, you
can only become aware of it.
I refuse to believe that your fall was a fallacy. As a
sacrifice, you went where you went, only to show us
how far we could go, with all of your potential

& the marrow of life on your tongue.

We learned of body-awareness.
Our wings, of course, are our bodies.

Our wings didn't fail us. We had every bone &
muscle in attention except for the mind where we
were intoxicated by grief.

We were invisible except for the images of our selves
on screens, heroic in our delusions.

I've been dealt enough aeolian barbs.
I've seen them come at me with dark velocity
with Roman limbs
with svelte plead & dire zephyry.

Why did your Spring come at me so sprung?
Like that slipped disk that flung out (like you were
thrown out) silhouetted in the red of nerve, the red of
ache & burn & with some burning *why* in its calcium
its muttering still raw,
its muttering, so rapid a roguery

—just tell me, as I pull out my lyre…

Does this blue dementia glide?
Will this glimpse of you surrender?

& if I, with an unquenched it of handsomeness &
dreams, am, unapologetic—& in this so-called lilt of
my it, I'll walk alone with spiders & drink & drink to

the charm & the wit; this swagger, a gesture of freshly
smile & *(one more please…)* wearily,
I'll watch the buds brew.

Kind & malleable are the walls I've jousted with—
I made my mark of anonymity.

(& those saviors, who belly-flopped into that
next-world, a kind of place without this
woebegone & filth,
without this
            collection of muscle & spill
—what mass…
broke that delicious fall
& un-broke the mind…)

As engines whine in petulance, that very surreal
animal place is moseyed upon,
a paradisiacal place, ungated.

—but death is kind when it is not being chased
& it bears some kind of tongue-in-cheek demand—
as in, the ultimatum: fear, or love
such a nasty little question:
would you accept fear if it accepted you?

& I, spidery to touch, come with fingers & eyes
& I, will crawl again—into the evermore of leisure.

What can we do for arachnophobes but teach them
to love the tickle, then feed their quench?

I took the wheel with eyes closed & assumed the road,
feeling for my arrival in my perceptions.

Later at the trial, the honorable, Infinity, ruled against
me & gave kitten-eyes to Velocity on the stand…

(we only shared some minor nirvana between us)

—we had one thing on our minds:
the drip of oil becoming constant.

Our bodily gestures merely exhibited a remorse for
the fleeting tock of time.

But Icarus,
in this mongrel-hug disguised as a solace
I'm comforted by the ought of rhyme,
yet somehow, I'm aliened…

I notice, "runaway," on the lips of a shore & sure,
I put it there, as to seem Genuine, traveled by some
lure of a revolt & jibe.

It is so mechanical for me to conduct these
grammarian flaws in the fine-print, the smudging
that is my name on this *Bildungsroman*
with a future of uncertainty
somewhere in the self & serif.

So, say, turbines give us our daily sneak,
but the truth of bread & a crying babe is plain
we're hollow in this meaty war, with faces left out
in the sun, wrinkled

daily is this creak: same stalling, spitting engine
moving on down the runway,
same shadows growing tinier & tinier.

The ingenuity of a worm's moveability comes from
pain, hunger.

That daily sneak, with that tote of dreams, clinched.

This frankness, this illegitimate cry for something
more than its few, its few rationed spouts of err &
make; its makings in the hoot-owl school of
doomspeak & frank.

This frankness, this rib of tomorrow's birth (minor
imitation, minor melody) is only a rain of drown &
spark

& the words which were puddles are now resounding
bangs, or a freedomhood, freed.

Icarus, just as your situation grew cantankerous in the
vague sudden…
I, too, made some verbalization, some announcement
(just as Odysseus arrived at Ithica with the smell of
Calypso's sex in every crevice… just as Sisyphus
stubbed his big fat toe…
I, too, know of migratory winds
& the rebels how they swarm,
so I put trust in myself & my bloodbeat).

—yet, how terrible it is, for the human race
to mutilate bald men's heads…

& I hear violins like tempest swells, or an overloaded
freight.

From a logicians stance, looking beyond
accumulations of land & sea, I very humbly refuse to
analyze the shall of this intuit & all the possible
treasure of her eyes, moreover, bricks like religion &
ought like fire—moreover, flame like hurt like prettily
scorn—moreover, distinguish like a sorcerer's
jadishness—moreover, things like memory like suffer;
I very humbly direct these two eyes
onto your forsake-me pose:

how in the end, it was nothing but a droplet.

I come to you bearing hypotheses:

Distance + Time

Fictions & Hope

& I am curious about
feathers & glue

I am curious about
the birds

how they glide along the ocean's surface
immersed in reflection

I am curious about meatbombs
& musical breaks:

the flautist's speed-gouged solo
          accompanied by this
crust of Earth...

that doctored venture
thru moods
reliant on ticks
& clangs.

I, too, descended
when the jazz became too much for me
too altitudinous with Phrygian scales,
Aeolian scales,
distance & savagery.

I reached inside... into whims
where my *prana* was cozily detached,
malingering
                    where I once
malingered.

Icarus, didn't you find it strange
when the relative wind
touched you with indifference
& the whole mess of it all, all those instructions
disappeared from your mind?

I came to that office window, under fiery bowels
& manifested myself
to your heights
with suns & decreased density
with rich probable hands

with a vision
of importunity

with keenness
& bruised arms
holding your body
the way I held
all those other bodies,

their bodies, ruined
filtered thru aggressive winds & opinion

remembering how they once held Galileo's apple
with giddiness

how the serpent hissed,
cursed 'em all,
with ills, with a jackknife
thru the heart

riding a Cessna named, Desire.

Our happy windfalls, departed with a grin
pried from paleness
& the never-ending ache…

some subtle root of bone like language,
but not language, more so, the seem-so
of like-dreams:

the rise & lonesome nevering of a fall, or,
an offering, a solace in the tribulation,
which is something happy or nonhappy

in memories of the hurl
idling into tranquility
with something amiss…

(perhaps,) I was distracted throughout that sheepish
fall.

(perhaps,) I was distracted by the dirty colors of our
sky.

(perhaps,) I was distracted by our angel-headedness,
however giant, of wrath, & fiercely, swoopingly,
fallen—

(perhaps,) I was disturbed by our Prince, vomiting his
yesterday onto tomorrow's weather report.

Erratic are these bodies,

outlined in vertebraic zoologies…

somehow elusive,
emerged from nude silences—

Silences, as the root of all elegy

Elegy, as the melodic fuel

the rush & tumbled
                          atmosphere

that conjured this ink,
this imperfection.

Your father's tears
were staged in experiments
                of trial & error

the horizon… was it a toy?
or something actual?

Time appears again
in a moonish hue

so weird, how it slips
        upon our sides

so weird, how it
        slings & swings.

The clock's face:
Der Schrei der Natur
(the Scream of Nature)

the meaning,
lost

the spinsters,
lost

at a loss for hours // the minute recovery
begs of us

while erraticisms glide & refute
The Stoic's Essential Guide: tools for resilience &
positivity

At the heart of your descent
there must've been

                    something to cling to…
a tongue,
logic,
amazement,
science—

The chakra that gave you away
gave you up with a gracious hand
in careful, distinct
Muteness.

Your body, uncensored
reeling with watery fortune
& frolicsome agony.

Breath of your breath
                mew'd up
is tingled
by steepness & plunge.

                —((*poetic carcasses adrift*))—

In my mind's eye
        there is a statuette
of your fall
(your bareness; that in-
tangible crisis)
& then there is
the divine sensation of lift.

Our primitive neurons, sometimes
show us
magic in dark hearts
deliverance in our hungers
Excalibur, as that
          muscle & flesh—

This nervous system,
violated by
conscious neglect,
imagination & ought.

Your arched agility, or
ooze of
          blue annihilation.

At the sacral slope,
               where sits the mammalian desire
          (sensations of wind on flesh, flesh on flesh)
—*Did you?*
Push your hips forward & arch into the vertical
contradiction // that mesh of language, crushed—

Or, at the sacral slope, the pulse, [*that makes calamity
of so long life*] sensations a-bound for eruption

—decisions, hard on the body.

If I am so symbolic, bred unto a body of thought,
a body of fear & un-fear, revolutionized by a feather,
by a father—our father—of ingenuity & fledge.

Then, with limitlessness undiscovered

Close your eyes…   breathe…

Sometimes I close my eyes & I am there in those
moments of bliss.

My material possessions: my bones, my intellect.

The future… the landing… was unthought of
it was needless to think of the future
only in the Now, self-reliant & in control did our
transcendence manifest.

Only then, did we go beyond our mammalness…
detached from Earth & all her rules; the timestamp
she forced upon our moments—we tried to look past
that. But in the end, Time, we could not escape.

I put the dirt in my hands
& I know something
I know why you broke the vow
between flesh & Earth.

Sincerely,
your frivolous apprentice.

Notes

Preface References:

Vladimir Mayakovsky, "Jubilee," *'Vladimir Mayakovsky' & Other Poems* (trans. James Womack)
Thomas Pynchon, *Gravity's Rainbow*
Michael McClure, "Revolt," *Meat Science Essays*
John Milton, *Paradise Lost*
William Shakespeare, *Hamlet*
Barbara Guest, "The Shadow of Surrealism," *The Durer in the Window*
René Magritte, *Selected Writings*

The line in "Blue-Eyed Napoleons": *thou comst in such a questionable shape*, is taken from William Shakespeare's *Hamlet*, Act 1, Scene IV.

"A Win(d)some Dedication" is for Saint Juan Diego Cuauhtlatoatzin, a Marian visionary (1474-1548).

"Flight, in Memoriam" is inspired by the following Leonardo da Vinci quote: "Once you have tasted flight, you will forever walk the earth with eyes turned skyward. For there you have been, and there you will forever long to return. "

"Naked & Fallen" is inspired by Bruegel the Elder's painting, *The Fall of the Rebel Angels*, as well as John Milton's *Paradise Lost*, and William Blake's *Marriage of Heaven and Hell*.

"Moloch's Fingers" refers to Moloch as one of the rebel angels depicted in *Paradise Lost*, but also Moloch as depicted in Allen Ginsberg's "Howl," in particular, the line:

Moloch, whose fingers are ten armies.

Sortie D'urgence is French for emergency exit.

The phrase, Dark-Vowelled Birds, is taken from the last lines of
Dylan Thomas's "Especially when the October Winds":

> *The heart is drained that, spelling in the scurry*
> *Of chemic blood, warned of the coming fury.*
> *By the sea's side, hear the dark-vowelled birds.*

In this book, Dark-Vowelled Birds symbolize skydiving
instructors.

"Beast of a Feather" is dedicated to the memory of Michael Suter
and to everyone who lost their lives in the Skydive Fox Glacier
plane crash on September 04, 2010, in New Zealand.

The haka from "The Rest of You" may be translated like this:

WHAT IS DEATH
IT IS LIFE
IT IS LIFE
THE HOLY POWER
TO FLY
TO THE TOP OF THE EARTH
WITH LOVE FOR THE GOOD LIFE
THE GOOD LIFE

"An Open Letter to Icarus" alludes to Pieter Bruegel the Elder's
painting, *Landscape with the Fall of Icarus* (1560), and the poem
of the same name written by William Carlos Williams.

The line in "An Open Letter to Icarus": *that makes calamity of so
long life*, is taken from William Shakespeare's Hamlet, Act III,
Scene I.

Acknowledgments

Thank you to all my fellow alumni of the Jack Kerouac School of Disembodied Poetics for all of your suggestions on this project, and to all staff and faculty at Naropa University with a special thank you to Jeffrey Pethybridge, whose guidance and support on this book is greatly appreciated. Thank you to these skydiving dropzones and the people that run them: the Parachute Center in Lodi, California, Skydive Franz Josef in New Zealand, and Rocky Mountain Skydive in Colorado.

On the front cover, the figure at top left is Icarus from Jacob Peter Gawy's *The Fall of Icarus* (1635-1637), the figure at the top right is a rebel angel from Pieter Bruegel the Elder's *The Fall of the Rebel Angels* (1562), at the bottom center are the following people from left to right: myself, Tommy Miller, Adam Chamberlain, Carlos Rodriguez, and Brockton Reich. Photo by Ben Nelson. Thank you to those skydivers for allowing to be on the cover, and for keeping it tropical.

I want to show appreciation for the following poets: John Milton, Michael McClure, Barbara Guest, Yusef Komunyakaa, Dylan Thomas, William Shakespeare, Allen Ginsberg, William Blake, Hart Crane, E.E. Cummings, Robert Duncan, and William Carlos Williams.

This book was formatted, designed, and typeset by the author in 12 pt. Adobe Garamond Pro typeface.